Faith Made

Well

Pressing to Believe
after losing my babies

Felicia Stevenson

Dedication

This book is dedicated to my husband, Tyrone Stevenson. Thank you for loving me and supporting me in this amazing journey. Thank you for being there every step of the way, holding me down, even though you had your own pain you were facing. You wore your emotions well just to support and love me the way Christ loves the church. Love you, T! And, to all my children, they are God's reward to us. I love you and thank God for each of you always.

Acknowledgement

This journey has been tough to walk, but thankfully I haven't had to walk it alone. When you are faced with obstacles and things that seem utterly impossible, having people in your corner is one of the greatest gifts from God. And, it never has to be a whole bunch of people. Not everyone is meant to walk with you. Sometimes, all you need is a faithful handful of God-sent people that are willing to walk this walk with you, side by side and hold you down. So, I must acknowledge my "faith connectors" and my intercessors – they know who they are. I am so very grateful for my small circle, thank you all.

I also want to acknowledge my family, the Macks and the Mills, for holding it down in prayer and support always. I'm grateful that you were all there for us with whatever we needed. Thank you because you didn't hesitate to join us in our faith walk throughout every trial. We love you and appreciate you all very much!

A letter from the author

For women who want to bring forth a child; but, were told they couldn't. I know exactly where you're at, and I have written this letter from my heart specifically for you.

Dear Brave Woman,

I want to share with you that you can and will overcome. My book is not an exact science; it has no fancy or magical powers to getting pregnant. This is my story, my testimony of faith, and the manifestation of God's promises in my life. And, I want to share everything I have gone through, suffered, learned, and done because if there is one thing I know is that God is not a respecter of persons. He does not play favorites. It is His will for us to produce children, to fill the earth, to walk in dominion and authority (Genesis 1:28).

This is my story of how hard it was for me to believe, to press, and to consistently get in His word. It was not easy, I cannot promise it will be easy. I can't promise you that you will birth a child or when it will happen. There is only one Miracle Worker. But, I can promise you God is faithful, He does listen, and He does work miracles. I can promise you that all things are possible to them that believe because God's word says it (Mark 9:23).

Get in His word and work the Word! Husbands and wives, stand together in agreement, ask God together and believe together. There is true power in agreement (Amos 3:3)! And, no matter what, count it all joy. Walk in faith. Believing and walking in faith are key; prepare for what you are believing and watch God work.

Love: Felicia

Opening Thoughts

I decided to name this book "Faith Made Well" because for most of my life, I felt like the woman with the blood issue (Mark 5:25). She had a condition for twelve years, went to doctors, and no one had answers. No one could help her, and she was getting worse. But, when she heard about Jesus, that all changed. She believed that, if she could just touch His garment, she would be healed. Like her, I had my condition for ten years, but I also believed that God could make me well. I applied my faith to make me well. My faith in Jesus would make me whole. I received so many bad reports and heard so many discouraging stories, I knew that my story was like hers.

Pushing past those reports, those voices telling me I couldn't have babies, and those faithless moments was like the woman pushing past the crowd of people who were in the way of her getting to Jesus. They were in the way of her healing. But, she wasn't letting anything, or anyone get in the way of what she believed. She *pressed* her way! And, I had to press my way!

In Mark 5:34 NKJV, Jesus tells the woman, "Daughter, your faith has made you well. Go in peace, and be healed of your affliction." When He says that, He is telling us that that is what faith does. It heals and makes people whole again. And, not just physically, as that would be a small thing for faith. Faith heals us inside and out and it completes us in God. This really resonates with me because I am living proof that faith in Jesus truly heals.

So, in sharing my story for His glory, I just pray that women everywhere will be encouraged to use their faith and continue to press through the crowd of negative reports, discouraging words, and disheartening circumstances. And, not just in birthing, but in every area of your life. Regardless of the bad report, you can also apply your faith, work the Word, believe God will do it, and He will. I hope my book blesses you and empowers in your journey, too.

Introduction

My name is Felicia Stevenson. I'm 38, and this is my story of learning about faith. First off, let's just say Felicia means "happy one", but I haven't always been happy. Then again, who has? Growing up I have always been a childcare provider. I remember being in the 2nd grade, taking my dolls to school, and while I did my classwork my doll would be on my lap; and I would rock her to sleep. I have always had a dream and desire to be with and work with children. My mother was in the childcare field, so it has always been in my blood. I watched her and babysat a lot. Caring for kids was second nature to me. It was such a pleasure and always a joy to watch them. I became a godmother at the age of 20. I was the primary caregiver for my goddaughter, and by the time I was 21 years old, I went through the Kinship Program and cared for five children under that program. It was truly a blessing. Over the years, I always had someone's child with me and I would shop and provide for them as if they were my own.

Kids. Kids made my heart happy and full. I never really did the dating thing because I was always around kids. They were my life. But, in 2003 I met Tyrone Stevenson. At first, he was just my friend, but soon after he became my husband. He was a single father of 3 children at 33 years old, and the primary caregiver for one of them. But, he also provided for the other 2 a lot. So, I became a stepmother to Tyrone Jr., Tenae, and Tiffani Stevenson; but let's just say I was a mom. Now, at the age of 15 I was told that I couldn't have babies, so the dream of giving birth was just a thought buried deep in my heart. But, the more I cared for other children, the more I wanted to birth my own. And, since I was married, typically next comes the readiness to have a baby, and we attested I was ready. However, I never really thought much about it because of what I had been told at 15. Therefore, I never brought it up.

So, here I was, preparing for my wedding; happy and excited about this man, Tyrone. Excited about how I get to spend the rest of my life with him. The morning of my wedding, I remember oh so well the butterflies in my stomach, the loss of appetite, the fear, and my list goes on. Nonetheless, my wedding went on; and everything was beautiful. I was in full expectation of the honeymoon only to end up terribly sick the whole time. I couldn't eat anything, and I felt horrible. I thought maybe it was just the excitement of my new life with my husband. Or, maybe it was due to the surgery I had undergone a month earlier. Maybe it was a side effect from the surgery, or maybe I had moved too fast and not taken time to recover properly.

Well, I got married on September 13th and, on October 10th, I found out I was pregnant! I was in total shock! I thought, 'No way, this just can't be.' How could I be pregnant? The doctor said I couldn't possibly be, but after four home pregnancy tests, two doctor's visits, blood work, and an ultrasound; it was confirmed. I was pregnant! My heart was overjoyed, as I thought about being a mom. I just couldn't believe it. After what doctors had told me from my teenage years, I was expecting my first child.

On my 3rd visit to the doctor, I received the news I had feared. The doctor said it was a high-risk pregnancy, and he went on to explain that my cervix was extremely short and thin, not capable of sustaining the embryo. "We don't think you will be able to carry the child, Mrs. Stevenson," were his words to me as my heart sank in disbelief. My heart was completely broken. I felt like I was 15 all over again, hearing the words of the doctor who told me I could never have a baby. I would go to church and I would pray, but I never really had faith. I didn't understand that our faith experiences serve to know what God is doing, what He is truly about.

I was placed on mandatory bedrest at 4 months pregnant. Absolutely no moving, I had to keep my feet elevated all the time, confined to my house day in and day out. It was week 24, and I thought I was going to lose my mind. I couldn't stay in my bed any longer. I went out just to visit my mom at a church event where I made sure to sit with my feet up. I thought so long as my feet were elevated, and I was sitting, all was well. But, bedrest means bedrest, and the doctor's instructions were not to be taken lightly. As I sat in the church, I could feel a drop down there and it freaked me out. So, I went back home shortly after. I laid down on my bed waiting for my husband to get home from work.

Two hours later, I was back at the hospital and placed on a monitor. The doctor had informed me that I was going into labor. At 24 weeks, going into labor. They rushed me to another hospital near by because the hospital I was in could not deliver a baby at 24 weeks. The whole ride, I remember crying and being scared, hearing the doctor's words resonate in my mind. "You won't be able to carry full term."

When I arrived at the hospital, I was a complete mess. I laid in the hospital bed for two whole days, tilted up in the air, trying to hold on to the baby for as long as I could. But, my baby was ready to be born. Twenty-four weeks. In my mind and in my heart, I was crushed. All my dreams and desires were coming down. I couldn't help but think that I was never going to be a birth mom. I felt like a failure, like it was all my fault for getting up and going to that church event. I was supposed to be on bedrest, but I didn't listen. I caused this; I put this on myself. And, because of my disobedience, I was losing my baby.

As I stared at the ceiling of this cold and bright room, I remember hearing my husband, sister, and doctor tell me to push. "Push, push," were the faint words in my ear, but I wasn't feeling it. I wasn't ready, I wanted my baby to stay in just a little while longer. 'It's too early,' I thought, 'not yet, it's too early.' I heard the doctor say once more, "Push!" And, so I did. Out came a tiny little baby; no cry, no noise. Just a tiny, little, still and small life.

Chapter 1

Tylisha: My Miracle

My baby was here! Weighing in at only 1 lb. and 8 ounces, this tiny little girl had only a 20% chance of survival according to the doctor. I was only 23 years old with a tiny baby. I was scared. I never even got the chance to look at her before she was immediately taken to NICU. But, I also never went to see here there. I thought, since she was going to pass away anyhow, it was better not to develop a bond with her. Her medical report was long; stemming from brain problems, bleeding, seizures, low heartbeat, to breathing abnormalities. It seemed everything was going wrong with my child, and I didn't want to see that. I didn't want to see my baby girl suffering.

Three days had passed, and I was still in the hospital, still had made no contact with my daughter. I kept thinking, 'Why is she still here?' I thought maybe she was waiting...for me. Maybe, she was waiting to see me. So, I rallied up the courage to visit my baby. All I can say is, once I laid my eyes on her sweet little face, it was love at first sight for sure. It was as if, the moment I looked at her, every opposing word about me being a mother had dissipated. I felt a spirit of boldness filling my heart and I realized, in that moment, that I was a mom. And, my fight had begun. Every negative thought I had was deleted from my mind. All I knew was that this tiny little being needed me, and I needed her.

Our newfound journey had begun. My husband and I started praying together and reading the Bible together. We understood this was out of our hands, and we needed God. We needed this God we had heard about for years; but, where was He? Where was God in all of this? Day after day, my baby's health kept declining. She was getting worse, and now her chances had dropped from 20% to 10%. The doctor would continually call us into meetings, urging us to just "let her go." And, it would have been easy to make the decision to let her go, but no. We weren't going to do that.

Instead, I called my grandmother who, in our family, is the prayer warrior. I told her exactly what was going on, and that we needed her to pray for our situation and our baby. And, she asked me a significant question that I will never forget. She asked, "Felicia, do you want your baby to live?" I said yes; and she told me to get in my closet, get in front of God, and tell Him. She said, "Just believe and trust that God will let her live." "How, grandma?" I replied. And, she just repeated to get in my closet and talk to God. I needed to tell Him what I wanted Him to do.

And, that is exactly what I did. I was at the Ronald McDonald House, and even though it wasn't my closet, I went into a closet to talk to God. When I did everything was getting worse, but this time, I had a sense of peace that it was all going to be alright. I couldn't explain it, but I felt everything was going to get better.

Sight wise, my baby's little body was getting tired. Her lungs were tired, her heart rate was dropping, and she was leaving us. At one point, she did go, but the doctors brought her back. The doctor called Tyrone and me into a meeting with several other doctors, each one giving their report on how our baby girl was declining. They proceeded to inform us of what was happening with her body and its growing weariness. They continued to press that removing the ventilator and letting nature take its course was the best decision for her. But, there was no way. At that point, I had become bold enough to stand up, with tears in my eyes, and say, "No!" I asked them for three more days to see what happens. I had gone through too much to let go now and, with a renewed strength, I was prepared to believe that my baby would survive this.

"Please," I said, "let's give it three more days. Please don't remove any of her machines yet, and don't do anything without her father or me being here." For the next three days, I knew the battle was on. I prayed and talked to my baby girl. I knew this battle was not just about her; but it was God's way of showing me something. There was something He wanted me to witness, something I had never seen before. Day 1, I stayed at the hospital all day and through the night, never once leaving my baby's side. Day 2, she started shaking profusely, and the doctor said this was just what they knew would happen. But, I held on stating that it was only day 2. There was still one more day to go.

Day 3, my belief was stronger than ever. I was speaking to my baby's body, every organ, every cell, every nerve, and every machine hooked up to her. I looked up all the cells we have in our bodies and every bit of her body make-up, so I could call them by name. I would sing to her and talk to her, making sure I told her who she was designed to be; who God designed her to be. In my time there, I would talk to and encourage the nurses on duty. I continually told them about the miracle they would witness through my daughter. With each conversation, I was getting stronger in my faith; and, I was able to laugh with and encourage other mothers in the NICU. I knew it was a set up by God!

In my heart, I knew God wanted me to go through this experience early in my life for a reason. I had always heard about God, but I had never experienced Him first hand. I had never seen who God was. And, now it was Day 3, and I was about to see the God everyone else talked about for myself. Right around 2:00 am, my baby girl's health started turning, and her heartbeat was getting stronger. Her numbers were going up, and the machine was producing positive results. All was looking good. It was all turning around just like I knew it would!

I was more excited when even the doctor said everything was going well; and he said, "Let's keep our fingers crossed for better." No! No fingers crossed, this is ALL God! On Day 4, my baby girl was doing so much better. I went to my room to rest a little, and my husband called me suddenly to let me know that her brain was bleeding. Instantly, I told my husband to step it up, speak to her body, and believe God to stop the bleeding. I knew it was the enemy attacking her because I had left, but what the devil doesn't understand is that my husband and I are one; and we are in this fight together. My husband picked up right where I had left off; and, by the time I arrived, the bleeding had already stopped.

Looking back, our journey was filled with ups and downs. There were many lows, but there were also a few highs. Yet, through it all, everything I experienced taught me to hold on even when it looks like it's over. I learned that I have the authority and power to call things into existence. Yes, I had heard about God and I knew about Him; but I didn't know Him personally until I went through all of this. And, when it was all over and

Tylisha came home four months later at 4lbs and 8 ounces, even with breathing machines and severe medical conditions, I could say that I knew and saw God. It was no longer hearsay; I had experienced His miracles and witnessed them firsthand. But, little did I know, that this journey of birthing and believing was only the beginning of God's hand over my life. We won! We were back home with our first baby. All was well. However, a month later, we were back in the hospital. This time the attack was even worse. It was as if everything we had already gone through was starting up all over again. A repeat of our four-month nightmare, and I still believed it was my fault. I must have done something wrong to be going through this again, right? 'I must have fallen off track somewhere,' I thought. The guilt was a terrible feeling.

But, I am truly thankful for the awesome husband God gave me. My husband kept reassuring me that it was not my fault. He kept saying that it wasn't me, but it was time to really trust God with everything. Because we had won the battle, we had gotten lax on declaring His promises. It was time for us to learn the power of agreement; and trust Him regardless of what was going on around us. So, that is exactly what we did.

Chapter 2

My Angel Baby: My Healing

One year into my marriage, and I was learning to be in constant agreement with my husband. In my first year of marriage, I had become a birth mother; and I was learning to trust God with my child's life. This time around, she stayed in the hospital for two weeks, with ups and downs throughout. But, when Tylisha came home, she was great. There were no medical problems at all. Not one. We stayed in New Jersey for two years and had decided to move to Maryland for a chance at a better financial life. Moving to Maryland was a great step, we thought, but we had no idea it would launch us into yet another faith journey.

When we moved, we were almost immediately able to find work, a church, and a place to call our own. I went back to babysitting, after all, caring for children was embedded in my heart. I became a "mommy" instantly not just to my own beautiful daughter, but to many children I cared for. My love, my passion and my heart has always been for God's little children.

We had been living in Maryland for five years, and Tylisha was now seven years old. I had gotten pregnant again. Once again, a high-risk pregnancy. Another tiny baby rollercoaster ride. All these thoughts ran through my mind taking me back to everything we had gone through with Tylisha. But, this time, I was excited! Another baby, yeah! I would go to my doctor's visits and everything was fine. The doctor saw no problems with the baby. So, I thought this pregnancy would be normal. This would be truly a blessing from God. The blessing of having a normal pregnancy.

Every two weeks I would go to my doctor's appointments. The reports were always good, everything was good. And then, on my tenth week visit, the ultrasound showed no heartbeat. They said the baby was gone. No heartbeat. That day they sent me home and told me to return the next morning for a D&C procedure (dilation and curettage). 'Wow,' I thought, 'just like that? It's over?' I cried like a baby asking the Lord why, how could this be? I begged Him to put a beat back in the baby's heart. I remember pleading with the Lord. I was upset, scared, and questioning; 'God, why?'

Thoughts of what the doctor said popped back in my memory. Thoughts of my inability to carry a baby. I can't hold a baby was my only thought pattern. Before the night fell, I had miscarried. We had company that night, and I remember the terrifying feeling of embarrassment as I bled everywhere. I was crying; upset, scared, and completely lost. They took me to the hospital and, suddenly, it was all real. I thought to myself, 'you really lost the baby.'

As the reality of my loss set in, I kept consoling myself with thoughts of my Tylisha. Oh well, God blessed me with one. I should just enjoy her when all of this is over because as the doctor said, I cannot carry a baby. So, at least God blessed me with one, right? Who was I to ask for more? To expect more from God? Instead, I should be thankful for the one; that is what God gave me.

By thinking that I should just stick with the one, I was suppressing what was in my heart. I gave up on having another child even though I really wanted one, and my husband did too. But, I settled on the belief that God allowed me to have one. She was alive and healthy, with no medical problems. What more can I ask for after going up against all odds with her? I should just enjoy the baby God blessed us with.

Because I kept telling myself that, and saying it out loud, everyone else started saying it too. All my friends and family would repeat it over and over. I had settled, so they settled. My favorite expression they would use was, "God did what was best and He makes no mistakes." So, what? Does God want me to feel this way? Does God want me to be down and brokenhearted? Friends and family came over and surrounded me, and for a few, it felt good. But, once the crowd left, thoughts of my loss returned. Could I possibly have another baby?

The next morning, I went in for the D&C procedure. The doctor told me that they would perform the procedure and do a complete cleaning, and everything would be good. She said my body would need to be cleaned out because there was "a lot going on with my uterus." Apparently, there had been a lot of residue left over from when I was pregnant with Tylisha, but no one had explained that to me before. My doctor assured me that after a month or two, we could try again. She said she didn't see why I couldn't have another baby and that she expected to see me again soon.

Her words had given me a glimmer of hope, and that is exactly how I walked out – with hope. I had a chance to believe again. Yes, it was going to happen again. I was going to have another baby. Thoughts of another baby overflowed in my mind, and I felt myself getting super excited. And, now, I *wanted* another baby. Now, more than ever, I had the desire for a second child.

Chapter 3

My Angel Baby: My Strength

Four months after my doctor's visit, I got pregnant again. In my mind and in my heart, I was having this child. After three tests, and a visit to the Emergency Room, it was confirmed. We were pregnant! 'Okay, God, let's do this,' was my immediate thought. I remember telling everyone about the pregnancy and how, this time, it was happening! I remember all the positive words and the great love I received from everybody. Their excitement for me ignited my own excitement! The Stevenson's were having another baby!

Three weeks later, I was back in the emergency room. I was spotting, and hours later, that spotting turned into full on bleeding. This led to another miscarriage. I had lost another baby. The hurt, the tears, the disappointment of not hearing a heartbeat again was too much for me to bear. My world was caving in, and I felt like it was all over. I was upset and lost, and my spirit was broken. I was completely over with life itself. I kept running through all the things I had done; maybe this was my punishment. I ran through every negative thought I had, thinking that was why this happened. Something I did caused this to happen to me...again.

I secluded myself and went into "hiding." I hid behind false thoughts of "being okay." I limited my thoughts to myself, my husband, and my daughter. I blocked out both miscarriages, never allowing myself to grieve. I prevented myself from thinking about it, and I fooled myself into thinking I was okay. I wasn't going to think about it ever again. I was fine. 'It's okay, God blessed us. He gave me a child. It's what I will accept. This is my family, and I am okay.'

In the midst of my pain and heartache, I had found a new church home. I knew I needed healing. It was at this church that my new walk with God began. I was learning how to develop a spirit of faith, the true definition of faith, and how to use my faith. I learned how to truly walk by faith. The biggest thing I learned from my church was how, by helping others, God helps you. I can testify, now, that what you make happen for others, God will make happen for you.

My church also taught me how to prepare for what I was believing God for. You would think this is minor, but faith is action. And, if you are believing God for something, then you need to do something that shows you are expecting. Preparing to receive and expecting He will do it. If you prayed, and you believe it's coming, you need to put His word to work. And, that is what I did. I was determined to put God's word to work in my life.

A friend of mine had told me about a book that dealt with pregnancy loss and how to continue believing God for a baby. I would look in the Bible for scriptures about barren women and write them down. I would study them and speak them over my womb every day. The pain was still very real, but my faith was strong. I started doing research on fertility, and I couldn't believe how many women were affected by infertility. So many women had my same story and shared my same pain. Wow. This whole time, I had felt so alone in my situation; but, the truth is I was not alone in my despair. I knew what I needed to do.

My heart was set on starting a group for women who had been through what I had been through. I wanted to make it a movement, give it a voice, if anything, for the sake of supporting and strengthening each other in our pain. It was the Faith and Fertility Group of Maryland. At first, we started in my living room, but the group grew exceedingly. It wasn't long before we had to move our group to the local public library. All the while, I was in this cycle by myself (or so I thought) and, as it turns out, others were in it too. It wasn't just my story anymore. We all shared our pain and cofound a renewed strength and belief in God. Through God's word, I became a big "faith walker", and my whole life had changed. I was starting to see God in a new light.

Every day, I applied the word to my womb. I had nine prayer warriors and a faith connector. My pastor, at the time, said in one of his messages, "If you're believing God for a baby, go buy baby clothes..." Faith in action. So, before I could expect a baby, before I could get pregnant; I started preparing for what I was believing. I went out to purchase small baby items and clothes. I rearranged my room to make space. I was getting ready and walking in faith. I had been at this for two months, preparing and working my faith. And, then...

Chapter 4

My April

I got pregnant! The manifestation of God's miracle in my life! And, this time I was not surprised because I knew it was my faith and God's response to it. It was all God. Considering this was my fourth pregnancy, and I had lost the last two, this pregnancy was considered high-risk as well. The doctor was monitoring this one very closely, which was fine by me because I knew this was a gift from God. I knew this was His doing; therefore, everything was good!

After two months of being pregnant, they started giving me shots to help me sustain the baby full term. At the end of my first trimester, the doctor found out that my cervix was extremely weak. As the baby got heavier, my cervix would get weaker causing it to open and get rid of the baby. This was the problem I had with my previous two pregnancies. But, none of the other doctors had been able to catch it ahead of time. Side note, when you're walking in faith, things will manifest in your life, not perfectly and not the way you expect exactly, but just the way God perfectly planned it.

My thoughts, 'Okay, thank You, Lord. Thank You for bringing this to our attention and the doctor's attention now. Thank You for bringing to light what was happening on the inside of me, so that it could get worked out.' God was giving me revelation of my situation and answering all my questions from the past. Now, I gained the understanding that it wasn't my fault. My miscarriages weren't caused by anything I did or did not do. It was the weak cervix.

Knowing about this problem, helped me to accept and understand why Tylisha had come so early; and, why I had lost my last two babies. It gave me an inexplicable peace in my heart. So, the doctor wanted to perform a special procedure on me called *cervical cerclage*. Cervical cerclage is also known as a cervical stitch. It is used to prevent the cervix from shortening or opening too early. Basically, they would go in through the vagina and place a string that tightens up the cervix, allowing it to hold the baby full term. It was truly amazing, so I wanted to pray on it. Yes, this was something we were going to move forward with.

I decided to get the procedure done and all went well, praise God! I continued preparing for my baby and speaking over my womb. I, also, made it my mission to encourage other women to hold on to their faith and press past the pain. I would encourage them to apply God's word and watch Him do it. I knew that if they believed with all their heart, He would do for them what He did for me. God is no respecter of persons and He doesn't play favorites. What He does for one, He will do for another; that is His word.

We were in full preparation mode, rearranging furniture and setting up gifts that were coming from friends and family. I was 20 weeks pregnant and everything was good! It was time to find out what we were having, boy or girl? I couldn't wait; and, when we found out we were expecting a girl, my excitement grew even more! Everything was happening just as God said in His word. In every visit, every ultrasound, every opportunity I was applying the Word. Seeing my baby girl grow inside of me was truly amazing. My husband and I would go to every visit together.

The Sunday afternoon before Thanksgiving, during church service, our Pastor called me up to the front. He knew all about what we had gone through and our faith fight, so he asked me to lay hands on the barren women of our church. So, I did, and I prayed for all the women who were believing God for a baby. I will never forget that service and the awesome move from God. The whole time I prayed, my baby was actively moving in my belly, as if she was in agreement with our prayer.

The following day, I went in to my doctor's appointment but, this time, things were different. My vaginal cerclage was opening in my body, and I was going into labor. The doctor scheduled me to come in on Thursday, Thanksgiving Day, for another cerclage surgery. This time they would stitch higher to sustain the baby better. I was on mandatory bedrest until then. Thursday morning, I went in for my surgery and it was seemingly successful. There were no issues and we were doing good, so I was discharged that night with mandatory bedrest for three weeks.

The next day, family and friends came over with food for a post-Thanksgiving Day dinner! What a joyous day I had. Even though I was in my bed, my room was filled with an abundance of prayers and love. We were all talking and playing the name game, it was all so exciting for me. I didn't want the night to end. Having everyone there was such a blessing, and I still had my baby girl. All is well.

November 29, 2012 – something was wrong. I felt it; pain, excruciating and all-too-familiar pain. In my pain, I started calling on the name of Jesus. I was speaking the word, declaring over my womb, but it only got worse. I was rushed to the emergency room and, when I arrived, I was instantly taken to Labor 3 Delivery. In my thoughts, I kept asking the Lord what was happening. And, worry began to creep in.

Four hours later, my doctor walked into the room, sadness written all over his face. I didn't understand it, though. I was on the monitor and I could hear her heartbeat. So, why the long face? "Mrs. Stevenson," he said, "your stitch was infected, and we have to remove it. If we don't remove it, you will get sick. But...when we remove it, you will go into labor. Your baby is already infected; and, she will not survive outside of the womb. I'm sorry."

My mind was racing. So, you're telling me I'm going to lose this child? No way. No, this baby was promised to me. This baby was from God, I know it. God says in His word that He blesses the barren woman. I'm not losing this baby. "This baby, I shall not lose. I shall not lose." I cried and just repeated those words over, and over again. My baby shall live and not die to declare the works of the Lord. My husband and I were crying out to God before going into surgery. We knew we were facing something that God was allowing for a reason. Lord, let Your will be done. After prayer, my heart was at peace and I felt better. I called the doctor into the room and told him we were ready for surgery. But first, I asked if we could pray with him, and he assured me that he was believing with me. So, with my faith on high and a heart filled with expectation of a miracle, I went in the operating room to get the stitch removed.

After the surgery, the doctor apologized to me profusely. "Don't be sorry," I responded, "sometimes we have to accept God's will even if we don't agree or understand it. This baby belongs to Him way more than she belonged to us." When I returned to the Labor & Delivery Unit, the labor pains began. I was in labor all night with powerful contractions, and I could feel my baby's heart beating the whole time. I called out to my sister, making every effort not to push, but the baby was making her way. My nurse came in around 5:00 am and told me it was time. She said my body was ready, and it was now time to give birth. As she held my legs and instructed me to push, all I could think about was my baby's heartbeat. In my mind, I kept telling myself she would surely make it, she was going to pull through, she would be my miracle #2. I looked over at my husband, with God-confidence in my eyes, and we were both in agreement that our baby was going to live. God promised us her and she was coming!

I will never forget that gasp of air she took, as she entered the world. They held her little body up for me to see, I took one look at my beautiful baby girl, then she dropped her little head. In that moment, my husband fell to the floor of the room, crying out to God. I had never seen him like this, but in my strongest voice I said, "What are you doing? Accept God's will, He loves us, and this is all His will. We have to trust Him." So, my husband stood up from the floor, with tears in his eyes, he held his daughter and said, "Thank You, Lord." He handed our baby to me and left the room. I held her tiny perfect little hand, and I thanked God earnestly for the 23 weeks He allowed me to have with her. I thanked Him for every appointment, every kick I felt, every craving I had, every ultrasound and bloodwork. In all things, His word says to give thanks; and, that is what I did. I held her all night long as I prayed. Then, we notified the rest of the family that our baby was gone.

The doctor and nurses had been in awe of my calm and peaceful response. And, I kept telling them I would see them next year. I was going to have a baby girl. I remember reassuring the nurse that I was okay, and that this was all a part of God's plan. Another nurse walked in to let me know that I would have to make funeral arrangements. At first, it was no problem; but then days went by. I was discharged and reality set in. I was back home, and I felt lost. Where was my baby? What happened? My sisters came over and planned the funeral, they handled all the arrangements for me. I just couldn't grasp what had happened. That day, I sat in the cemetery, staring at the whole in the ground, wondering. It's not supposed to happen this way. God promised me this child, so why was this happening...again? God set me up. He played me. Why was He allowing all this pain again? Why did He allow me to lose my April?

Chapter 5

Pain So Deep

After April's service and spending a few days with my family I finally had to go home. If you're reading this, you may know all too well what I'm about to say. The pain I had felt from these pregnancies was like none other. Constantly wrestling with the "what if's" and thoughts of self-hatred and self-blame. It was my fault. It was always my fault. Suffering through sleepless nights, physical pain in my body, and emotional hurt; I wouldn't wish this on my worst enemy. There were so many emotions running through me. Any plans I may have had for the future were subdued by a cold and overwhelming emptiness in my heart. I was lost, unsure if I'd ever find my way back. Unsure if I even wanted to come back.

And God? I was so angry at God. Why had He allowed this to happen? What was I supposed to do now? I felt betrayed by God, hopeless, faithless, worthless. Like I was less than a woman because I couldn't give birth. I couldn't do what a woman should be able to do naturally. Everyone around me would try to talk to me about God and encourage me to pray. Pray? For what? It was all in vain anyway. No. I don't want to pray. I tried that. I prayed for my baby and what did it get me? A room overflowing with baby stuff, but no baby. God had me preparing for this baby the whole time, knowing that I wasn't going to take her home. Why? Why all of this, God?

And, as if the pain of my loss wasn't daunting enough, my body was going through changes. I was producing breastmilk, and my agony only grew. Now, I felt like God was punishing me. This breastmilk was supposed to be for the baby; the baby He took. My sense of failure worsened. The pain was unbearable, and my sleep had gone from me. I couldn't sleep. I would see ultrasounds; and, I would feel movement in my belly knowing that there was no baby there. I would close my eyes and see my baby's face. When I saw pregnant women on television, the pain would flood right back into my mind. I replayed the labor over, and over again. Still feeling numb and in shock from it all. Still going through the event and what happened, why it happened; all while trying to pick up the shattered pieces of my heart.

I learned, quickly, that people don't really know what to say in situations like mine. Their heart might be pure, and they may mean well, but some of the things they would say to comfort me weren't comforting at all. And, when there's hurt, it's difficult to *say* anything that will heal it. Many people would either ignore what happened, as if it never happened; or tell me that God doesn't make mistakes. Who would want to hear that right now? So, was this a mistake? Was it a mistake that He "fixed"? They would say, "just enjoy the one God blessed you with." So, this baby wasn't blessed? They would tell me to move forward, but the problem was, I didn't want to. I wasn't ready to move on; I was still hurting. I had a baby, and that baby wasn't here with me. There are millions of people out in the world having babies they don't want, but the baby I wanted wasn't with me.

Why did I spend so much time in prayer and believing? Why would God do this? I felt so powerless, and I turned my thoughts to her. Did she feel any pain? Did she know how much we wanted her? Did she know how much we loved her? I was an endless fountain of tears as I could only imagine all these answers, but never knowing. I had felt a pain so deep, so excruciating, and so heart-wrenching; and I never wanted to feel this way again.

I was done and completely determined to never do this again. I was in too much pain, crying while everyone else moved on. Everyone acted like nothing happened. I couldn't keep repeating this cycle, I didn't have it in me. I love kids, and I've always helped others with their kids; so, I just couldn't fathom why this had happened to me. But, in my own struggle, I had a small circle pushing, praying and believing for me.

The best gift you can have in life is a circle of believers who will lift you up, even when all you want to do is stay down. I had a small group of nine women, very close friends of mine, who were fighting and pulling for me, despite my "giving up". They still believed God was giving me another baby. Before I tell you about what happened next, I want you to know something. Your circle, those closest to you, matters. Having people around you who are willing to use their faith for you when you've lost your own is significant. And, if you don't have that, get it because some breakthroughs in your life will come as a result of your intercessors.

Now, I have been completely transparent, and will continue to be. So, I pray you hear my heart when I say that, even though those great women prayed for me, there came a time when I stopped answering the phone. I stopped talking to them altogether simply because I didn't want to hear it. I didn't want to hear about faith, God and prayer. The only thing I wanted now was to go back home to New Jersey. I wanted to pack my things and move back to my familiar place where I knew I had family that would understand. Somehow, I thought that by moving, I would be okay. But, when I moved, the pain moved with me. It went wherever I went.

I had never experienced this kind of loss in my life, and I couldn't bear the cost. I was out of faith and I didn't understand where I was in my life. I didn't care what happened next. I was in a dark pit, in my valley. Brokenness was my new normal and this was my life. I did my best to be a good mother to my Tylisha, but my joy had gone away.

Chapter 6

My Reset

Then, one morning, I heard a distinct voice. It was God, I knew it was Him. It was as clear as daylight. I heard Him audibly. He said, "My word does not return back to Me void. If I said it, it will come to pass." I managed to utter two words in reply, "My child." And, He answered, "I opened your womb, and you will bring forth children." Did God just say *children*? My faith had awakened, and I felt as if my old self had come back. I was back walking in my dominion and authority, empowered and renewed. I had a second wind, and I was ready. It was like my whole life had been reset!

"Okay, Lord! I know You can, and I know You will give me a child," I kept saying it out loud. In tears, I would speak the word of God, pressing through any feelings of negativity. I had read that God bottles our tears, so I felt released to cry. I applied the word and walked in it with full confidence concerning my baby. I would take time to meditate and see myself pregnant. And, every time I would feel even an ounce of doubt creeping in, I would take my Bible and declare the word out loud. I would speak His promises and speak them over and over. I also had a prayer partner that would call me every week to encourage me.

And, then, "she" showed up. I met this woman that, unquestionably, was sent from God. She knew I had lost my babies, and she knew about my journey. When she came to visit me, she brought two large bins of baby clothes and baby items. And, she told me that she knew I was going to have a baby. When she said that to me, I just couldn't hold back the tears. I had wanted to buy baby items, but I thought that maybe I should wait. God gives us the desires of our heart when we delight in Him. It was like God had sent her to my door, specifically to reassure me that His promise was on the way.

I battled for seven months. As you might already know, it wasn't at all easy. There were times where I thought that maybe it really wasn't going to happen. There were times where both my husband and my daughter would say that maybe it wasn't happening. But, we would hold each other up in faith, knowing that God's promise was real. I would see other pregnant women, and I would sow into them. I would give them money and ask them to buy their baby something. I sent a box of diapers to another pregnant woman. I had been bitter before, but now, when I saw pregnant women I was excited for them. My joy was back! I was excited because I knew I was next! I was constantly planting seeds, sowing into newborns, and buying slippers for new moms. Every now and then, at night, I'd cry because I longed for my babies; but I knew they were in the arms of Jesus. I knew they had the best babysitter ever, their Daddy forever.

While we were in New Jersey, I got a procedure done called abdominal cerclage. This is different from the cervical cerclage I mentioned earlier in the book. I had to get this type of cerclage because of how weak my cervix was and my previous losses. The difference with the abdominal is that it is a higher incision in the abdomen that then reaches the cervix, and the cervix is stitched closed. It is permanent. We had been in New Jersey around family for some time now, and I was ready to go back to Maryland. So, we moved back to Maryland again! We found a nice place in a short amount of time, and my husband was back at work. Everything was back on track, it seemed.

Then…it happened. I had a positive pregnancy test! I was pregnant?! Thank You, Lord! It was all I could think. Thank You, Lord! I called the people who were praying for me and standing in the gap. The excitement came in like a flood, and I immediately knew I wanted to be back in New Jersey for this pregnancy. I know moving again sounded crazy, but I knew it would be different and would require a lot of doctor's appointments. I knew I would need to be surrounded by loved ones. I'd need help with my Tylisha as well. So, we didn't think twice. After only two months of living in our Maryland apartment, we were headed back to New Jersey.

Once we were back home, the appointments started almost immediately, and so did the bad news. The doctor started telling me how my body wasn't capable of carrying the baby full term, that my weight was a problem, and I should consider carrying up until 26 weeks. They said my cervix couldn't hold anything over 5 lbs. "Maybe we can let you carry up until 30 weeks, but it's not likely your body will be able to; your cervix is weak. And, it's just impossible," these were their words.

Oh, how those words brought so much joy to my soul. As soon as I heard them, all I could think was, 'with man it is impossible, but with God all things are possible.' I knew God was with me, and I was with Him. I delighted myself in the Lord, and I knew He would give me the desires of my heart. Bad report after bad report, my faith stayed strong. There were a few times where I'd see spots of blood, and the thought of losing my baby almost crept in, but someone would quickly give me a scripture to meditate on. Someone would offer me a gift of encouragement. My daughter would come home from school, rub my belly, and say that she had a little sister. I would tell her that we didn't know yet because it could be a little brother. However, deep inside, I wanted another little girl. But, I never said anything because I didn't want to seem ungrateful in asking.

I'd thank God for either a boy or a girl. Whatever He decided, I would be thankful, so long as the baby was happy and healthy. I wasn't going to ask for any particular gender. But, then, while reading the Bible, I saw that we *should* speak what we want. We should be detailed in what we're believing God for and not be afraid to ask Him for it. "Lord," I said, "I want a baby girl." I would speak it again and again. Soon, I was receiving items for girls! I was certain of it; I was getting a baby girl from God!

From doctor's appointments to mandatory bedrest to weekly shots, I did it all and my faith had never been stronger. I had made it to 6 months, and it was now time to find out my baby's gender! Part of me thought that I should wait, but I was so filled with expectation, I really wanted to know. So, that morning, I woke up praying and singing as I made my way to my appointment. The baby was kicking, it felt a lot like he or she was dancing which only added to my excitement. The excitement was so overwhelming, I had to pull the car over and step out. I thanked God as I cried, no longer tears of sadness, but of joy.

When I arrived, even the nurses were overwhelmed with excitement for me! The ultrasound technician had asked me what I wanted, and I said, "I told God I wanted a girl." And her reply was, "Well, He heard you. You're having a girl." Oh, my goodness! I could've jumped off that table as happy as I was! Thank You, Jesus! I had yelled so loud; I couldn't hold back. Then the doctor walked in the room and told me there was a problem. My baby was weighing down my cervix, and they needed to monitor me very closely. The doctor said he'd need to see me three days a week, and I gladly complied. I was going to be obedient and show up to every appointment, but I assured the doctor all was well because this was my reset.

Chapter 7

Joi: My Promise

Suddenly, everything seemed to start declining. It was like the devil was trying hard to make me doubt. He was trying everything he could to get me to faint and fold on my faith. But, no matter the report, I wouldn't bend an inch. Every bad report that came through, I just kept saying "all is well, all is well." In fact, the doctor was so used hearing me say that, he started saying it after all my appointments too! He would say, "All is well." And, then, we would both laugh overjoyed with confidence. Now, all the glory was for God, and it was up to Him.

I was eight months pregnant, February 26, and I was going into my regularly scheduled appointment. When they did the ultrasound, they said the baby was continuing to weigh down on my cervix and it could no longer hold her. They had to schedule an emergency C-section. Today? She had to be born today? It was the day before my birthday, and I really was not looking forward to spending it in the hospital. But, we know our plans are not always God's plans; and His plans are always better. God is always working things out for the good of those who love Him and are called according to His purpose.

My husband and I locked hands in prayer, and we called our prayer partners and closest family to pray for us. It was 3:00 pm, the doctor and nurse came in the room to let us know that in two hours I would be taken into the operating room. 'Okay, God. What's going on here?' I thought. Then the doctor popped his head back in the room, looked at me, and said, "All is well." Tears fell down my cheek, and I knew all was well.

All I could think was, 'It's all over baby girl.' I prayed and prayed, as I was just hours away from meeting her. I was going to be a mommy again. The hospital was filled with loved ones and happiness, expecting that soon I'd be holding my promise in my arms. Soon, I would be bringing my baby girl into this world, and everything that happened in the past was exactly there – in the past! Every bad report, every failed pregnancy, every heartache; it was all behind us. The doctor said my baby was just hours away from arrival! And, even though it was an early delivery, it was well with my soul. When the doctor did the ultrasound, it showed that the baby's weight was around 5lbs and 3 oz; and, my cervix was thinning, so they immediately moved me to the operating room. There was such a peace as the nurses prepped me, and we prayed. And, before I knew it, the doctor said, "Mrs. Stevenson, all is well. Meet your baby girl."

I could not praise God enough! I yelled, "Lord, I thank You!" The doctor looked at me and said that he's never had anyone say that after he's operated, but that it was good that I thank God because he didn't think it was going to happen! "Felicia Stevenson," he said, "guess how much she weighs?" I replied 5lbs, which was what the ultrasound reported. And, he replied, "No, way. She's 6lbs and 6 oz. We didn't think your cervix could even hold 5lbs; but, look at you! You carried over 6lbs!" We both laughed. Look at God!

Meanwhile, in the lobby there was a huge praise party taking place. Laughs, praises and love filling up the waiting room from our prayer community and all who believed God with us. God is truly faithful. My baby girl was here, and we thought it was appropriate to name her Joi. It was so fitting because she gave us back our joy. As the expression goes, "this joy we have, the world didn't give it, and the world couldn't take it away"! It was beyond happiness because happiness comes and goes. This Joi (joy) was forever. Of course, the enemy was upset with us, and he started attacking Joi's body. But, this time I knew better. I knew who I was in Christ Jesus; I knew she was God's promise to me; I knew this attack wasn't about her; I knew the devil only comes to steal, kill and destroy; and I knew everything concerning Joi was well. So, the enemy can take a backseat on this one because he picked the wrong one.

I was certain that if I had been placed in NICU, it was for a reason. It was for someone who needed us to encourage them and show the love of God. There was no doubt in my mind that if God had allowed this, it was so we could help someone else. And, sure enough, we met so many disheartened families. God even gave us the privilege and honor to lead a couple to Christ. See? This whole attack wasn't even about us. It was for God's glory! Afterwards, I remember asking God for the opportunity to stay in a room with my baby. I had never experienced being in a room with my newborn baby or leaving the hospital with my baby in my arms. As you might recall, my baby Tylisha was born very early and had to stay in the NICU at the hospital. So, the nurse had an extra room, and she let me stay the whole week in the room with my baby! That's favor! When Joi was discharged, I was so excited and grateful to God that He had granted me this desire in my heart.

When we returned home, the following day, we hosted a "Baby Welcoming Shower." And, we were blessed with so many gifts, and visitors from all over New Jersey, Virginia and Maryland. People came from everywhere to see Joi, and we were so humbled and grateful. They came with tons of baby items, more than we could ask for. Every seed I had sowed was returned to us a hundredfold. We were blessed beyond measure and these blessings, we know, were meant to be a blessing to others. So, the Holy Spirit reminded me of the families in NICU whom I had met, and I knew they couldn't afford baby items. So, we decided to bless those parents at the NICU as well. And, all the glory goes to God!

Raising Joi was a blessing from day one. From even before she was born, we didn't have to buy anything for her out of our pocket. She had everything she needed and then some. God has truly been Provider for both Joi and Tylisha. I was so thankful to see my girls growing, and to see all that God was doing in Joi's life. I thanked God for allowing me to celebrate every month of her life, every milestone. She was mommy and daddy's prayer answered. Soon, we moved into our own place. Every time I look at her, I smile, knowing that her story had impacted many, including myself, and would impact so many more. Her first year of birth was amazing; she was a fun and beautiful gift from God. She is a joy to us and many others. At two years old, she was still being blessed by people. And, her story was and is still blessing others. In conversation once, I turned to my husband and said, "Let's have another baby." It was just a thought that popped in my head, and he laughed and said it was up to God. I turned to him and said, "No, it's up to us. He gives us the grace and power. You know all we have to do is ask and be in agreement. I know we're just talking, but I really want a son." My husband shook his head in agreement, "Okay." Months passed, and we didn't speak of it again.

A year later, my father came to visit us. He looked at me in all seriousness and told me I was pregnant. And, he told me I was having a boy. I, instantly, replied that I was not pregnant. "I had a dream that you were pregnant, and you were having a boy," he said. I just thought, 'okay, dad.' I didn't give it another thought, and we went about our day.

Chapter 8

Nate: My Overflow

Well, I found out a month later that I was indeed pregnant. When I went to see my doctor, he looked at me and said, "Again? You want to do this to me again?" I laughed and said, "All is well, doc." He laughed too. I was ready, once again, to face all the reports and beat the odds. I was prepared to speak to my body. This was going to be an enjoyable pregnancy, and we were not going to go through any high risks, I believed it. My husband and I were in agreement, and we spoke life every day. Everything was on point, every visit resulted in good reports, no high-risk talk, no bedrest, and my cervix showed no issues. For the first time, I was truly enjoying being pregnant!

Every visit, the doctor kept saying that everything was going well, and that he was shocked that my body was taking this pregnancy so well. My baby was growing without any problems. But, of course, the enemy wasn't having it. Now, we were going through attacks on our family support and finances. But, God being God always covered us and provided for us. He never allowed us to lack anything. We had everything we needed.

Nine months flew by, and my baby was good and healthy. There were no problems the whole time. Four days before my scheduled C-section, we had planned a gender reveal party with close friends and family. I couldn't wait to reveal what we were having. It's a boy! Yup, just what I wanted! The Lord had granted the desires of my heart, a wonderful pregnancy and our baby boy. I went in for my scheduled C-section, and the doctor asked, "Mrs. Stevenson, are you ready?" I replied, "Yes, doctor," and he wheeled me back to the operating room. As he was taking me to the room, he asked me about this pregnancy. It was different than all the others, and he wanted to know what I did. I said, "It was simple. I asked God to let this one be a normal pregnancy. I asked Him to let me have the experience of being in the hospital room with my baby, no NICU." My doctor said, "You did?" And, I replied, "Yup, they might seem like small requests, but He listens to them all, and He answers my prayers." It was truly unbelievable!

So, my baby boy was born at 8lbs and 4 oz. He was a big, healthy boy and we went straight to my room. For the first time ever, I got to hold my baby and bond with him right after birth. Everything went well. God answered my prayer and gave me this bonus child to hold and love. Now, I felt my family was complete. But, if it was or wasn't complete, well that would be up to God. He is the One who can and will open my womb. I will allow His will to be done. I was just a thankful and grateful mommy. Although the whole journey was rough from the start, the reward is awesome! Faith makes things happen.

I believed God for each of my children. And, yes, I was knocked down several times; but, I got up and fought back with faith. My babies that aren't here on earth, are not lost. I didn't lose them, they're with Jesus and I will see them again. I have 3 angel babies that I know I will see again. So, for anyone who is in a faith fight like mine – barrenness. I want to tell you that God does hear us. You need to stay in faith. Don't readily believe the reports from doctors because they are men. God has the final say. Remember, He gave us the power to speak and change our situations. Speak life in whatever area you're believing God for. There is no secret to what God can do, and He has no limits. He can give you what you ask for and more! Stay in faith, pray without stopping, believe, and you will see.

Steps I Took to Believe

1. Renew Your Mind: I had to remove all negativity from my life. All the negative thoughts in my mind had to go. But, to remove negativity, I had to guard my eyes and ear gates. Your eyes and ears are the gates to your heart. Everything you see and hear form thoughts in your mind. Be intentional about what you're listening to, who is around you, and what they are saying.

2. Verbalize: I had to speak God's promises over my life. My words had to be aligned with God's truth. Use your mouth, your voice, your words. Speak life into your situation. Declare that you are the healed woman of God, that it is God's will for you to birth, that all things are possible to she that believes. Declare that He blesses you and increases you and your children.

3. Faith Connectors: I had to get some real faith connectors that were there to agree with me and pray with me. Everyone didn't need to know my situation, and everyone doesn't need to know yours. Get a small circle of "real deal" intercessors. Your faith connectors that will pray and intercede on your behalf and lift you up.

4. Visualize: I had to practice seeing myself pregnant. I saw myself claiming my victory. Take time to yourself. This can be meditation time in which you see yourself pregnant. Imagine your belly, your pregnancy glow, your baby's features, your baby's room. But, this works in every circumstance. Whatever you're believing God for, see yourself in it and having it, and it will happen.

5. Stand on His Promise: I had to keep God's promise before me. I stood on His promise, wrote scriptures down, and placed them around baby items. Stand on God's promises, write them down, and keep them close to your heart. God can do anything; but fail. He cannot contradict His word, and His word is filled with promises for you.

Things I Learned

I'm sure you are thinking, 'why me?' I know because I had all those thoughts, too. But, I am living proof that all things do work together for our good. No matter what it looks like and no matter what it feels like, God always turns for good what the enemy meant for evil. This was not a journey I chose. I didn't want to hear that I couldn't have children at the age of fifteen. It is not what I wanted, but looking back, it is what God knew I needed to have a relationship with me, to show me how much He loves me, and how amazing He is. In whatever you're facing, be open to learning. There is a lot I learned from my journey.

I learned that God is always in control and that His will is perfect. No matter what I might think, or anyone might say, He is the only One in control. And, I learned to talk to God. Not deep, but real. I talked to Him daily, and I would tell Him all the details even though He already knows it. He is concerned with every detail of our lives, especially with bringing forth children. I learned patience and trusting in His timing. Sometimes we see an easy exit or alternative or hear about a treatment that we think will work. Or, we just adapt to our situation. However, I had to learn to stay on track and trust Him fully because He has perfect timing and makes no mistakes. He does all things well.

I learned to trust in the Lord with all my heart and lean not on my own understanding (Proverbs 3:5). I learned to walk by faith and not by sight (2 Corinthians 5:7). No matter what you see, speak what you know about God's word. We have the power in our words to speak to dead situations and bring forth life. We have the power of agreement. Going through all this woke up in me the belief in God and His everlasting word. But, knowing the word, reading it, speaking it is not enough. We must work this word, intentionally. We must work our faith with action. It's what you do, your acts of faith in what you're believing God for, that makes the difference because faith without works is dead (James 2:26). So, I thank you for taking time to read my testimony, and I pray that this encourages you to go boldly and get all God has for you.

36639024R00036

Made in the USA
Columbia, SC
26 November 2018